*The Gethsemane prayer!* A prayer we must pray at some points in our lives as God's children. But really what is this prayer all about? Femi Jaiyeola, through this small but impactful book, sheds some light into what this prayer is. He goes on further to disclose why we need to pray the Gethsemane prayer—Thy will be done—even as we feel the pain, sorrow, and deprivations that may accompany the will of God.

Patience Udo

# The Gethsemane PRAYER

Femi Emmanuel Jaiyeola

LUCIDBOOKS

**The Gethsemane Prayer**

Copyright © 2023 by Femi Emmanuel Jaiyeola

Published by Lucid Books in Houston, TX
www.LucidBooks.com

Scripture quotations are taken from the King James Version (KJV): King James Version, public domain.

ISBN: 978-1-63296-985-9
eISBN: 978-1-63296-628-5

Special Sales: Most Lucid Books titles are available in special quantity discounts. Custom imprinting or excerpting can also be done to fit special needs. Contact Lucid Books at Info@LucidBooks.com

*This missive is dedicated to the triune God. God the Father, who has and designed His Utmost WILL, God the Son who went and gave us the example of yielding to the WILL of His Father, and the Holy Spirit from whom we get the ALL:*

*The Holy Spirit gives this inspiration that birthed each line in this piece. He is the comforter that comforts during the time of grief as He would do for all who are going through it now and anytime. The Holy Spirit is the teacher that teaches what to say and do in such a time. He is the guardian who guides actions. He counsels us when we feel so confused and distrust of what to believe or whom to trust and He encourages us at the time when we feel so downcast and send peace and the right words into to. Explains the mind of God He prays and helps us to pray at all times. He is so close and whispers gently when everyone is gone and asleep. He makes us understand when we cannot understand each other. He calms us as the dove of heaven. He sends energy into our hearts and keeps us on fiery lines just as the spirit of power that He is to be able to confront the subtility of the devil.*

*God bless you!*

# Table of Contents

# Foreword

The quest to achieve and the pursuit that ultimately follows is what introduced me to Femi Jaiyeola on a bright and sunny day in August of 2015. Arriving with his family and relocating to Pullman, Washington, Femi was on the last leg of his journey in achieving his long-sought desire which took him from Nigeria to the United Kingdom, and then to the United States, the receiving of his PhD.

Throughout one's lifetime we have the opportunity to encounter individuals and build relationships, some maybe not as strong as others, but as both parties contribute to a relationship, there becomes a strong tie that binds them together through the good and the not so good of times. I must admit though, when I first met Femi, it seemed as if I had found a long-lost brother I never knew existed. Our desires, the humor we shared, the pranks we tried to pull on each other, and our love for the things of God. Even though he was from Nigeria, he had to be my brother! His demeanor and zest for life and his zeal to integrate his life with those around him to help improve the quality of their lives lit a spark between us that allowed God to forge such a strong bond between us. But the bond didn't stop there. My wife and I were introduced to the rest of Femi's family, from Maria his wife, to Manny, Maria Jr, and on to Joshua his youngest, and to this day we share a unity and bond that, we thank the Lord, will never decay.

Even the best of brothers still had difficulties from time to time. Femi and I were no different in this department, but thank the Lord, not in a disruptive way. Femi, being from Nigeria, as one would expect, coming from another country spoke a different dialect, and communicating posed a problem as there were times that I just couldn't understand what he was trying to get me to understand. Our most memorable misunderstanding has to be the time he requested his "sticks." And yes, those of us who speak the English language fluently would agree with me that he was indeed requesting "sticks." Well, as the story would go, a couple weeks earlier, I had promised Femi that when I went to the meat market that I used for stocking up on meat products for our freezer, that I would bring back a side of wrapped rib-eye "steaks." If you're following along with this little story, I think you may already see where the problem is, but Femi met me before church and asked, "Where are my sticks"? Even after having him repeat himself 6 times, I still could not for the life of me figure out why he would want a handful of sticks. It was only after he took me by the collar to my wife, where he asked my wife where his "sticks" were. For some reason beyond my comprehension, it only took a moment for my wife to realize he was looking for his "steaks." The pursing laughter that erupted because of the miscommunication has been a staple in our conversations and gatherings ever since, and it still gives me great pleasure to hand to Femi from time to time a handful of actual sticks to remind us of the strength of being good brothers and the joy we share.

Eight years now, we have enjoyed the triumphs and disappointments of life as families. My wife and I were there for Manny's graduation from junior college, Maria Jr.'s graduation from high school, and the grandest of them all, Femi himself receiving his PhD. These were wonderful moments that you build your family and life upon, and along with God's guidance, what you use to plan ahead for the future, and the future was bright. Manny and Maria Jr. had moved along the east coast to their prospective locations at the colleges they were attending, Femi had received a job with his credentials, Maria had taken on a job, and Joshua was class president of his 12th grade. Yes, life was moving forward, and it seemed like it was all green lights ahead. On September 23, 2022, at approximately 12 o'clock noon, the phone rang in Femi's office, and answering it just like he would any other call there at work, in a moment of time, the voice on the other end of the phone completely disrupted his life, thoughts, and ambitions, and caused his world to stop turning. In the many years of studying, you would think that there would be a clear answer for all questions and situations that may face us, but with that call, all the years of schooling and preparation still did not equip Femi for the news that he had to digest in that moment of time.

Disbelief, horror, shock, and a virtual cloud of darkness came over my wife and I as the news was relayed to us of the tragedy that had taken place. Our only thoughts then were of how soon we could travel to be at the side of Femi and his family. If our hearts were this torn by the news, we knew our friends had to be suffering immense pain themselves. Upon arrival, there were only weeping and tears that we could share along with the long embraces to comfort our truly broken-hearted lives because there are no words that could have been spoken to relieve the pain and suffering. Lives that had been so happy and full, now deflated as an exhausted balloon, had to face the difficult voices that filled their heads with questions: How? When? Where? And the crushing one, why?

Where do I go from here? Every father who faces tragedy and finds that all the hopes and dreams that they had planned for their family have been crushed and derailed finds themselves asking that same question, and it was no different for Femi. Folks, I can tell you all that I know where Femi went. He went to the Lord, his Creator and Savior, and in the midst of him asking God "why," I saw how God began the healing process to restore and strengthen Femi in the days that lay ahead. In the studies of mythology, one of the myths that arises is that of the Phoenix, a bird reborn from the ashes of its predecessor. Well, I do not take any stock in the story and the mythology of the Phoenix though it makes an entertaining story, but what I do take stock in is the power of the living God and the transformation He is able to perform in the lives of His servants who put their trust and confidence in Him. I have seen God take my friend Femi and raise him from what would appear to be a pile of ashes to a life again filled with hope and great prospectives, but that is his story, and I encourage you to read through this book to find how, with God's help, He will bring forth "beauty from ashes."

Thanks for sharing your story and conquest with the world, my brother, and remember, the next "sticks" are on me.

*Lee Spakousky*

*Colfax, Washington State*

# Foreword

This book is a deeply spiritual, inspirational piece penned by Brother Olorunfemi Emmanuel Jaiyeola. This he did amidst severe sorrow occasioned by the sudden death of his 22-year-old firstborn son. I deem it a great honour and privilege to write a foreword to this book, not only because I shared in the grief of those dark hours, but also in the fulfillment of his request.

The book of Job in the Holy Scriptures, especially the 19th chapter, is a deep expression of grief arising from Job's hour of trial and loss. In chapter 19 verses 23 and 24, Job hoped that his words were written and printed in a book, and that they are graven with an iron pen and lead in the rock forever. Thankfully, God granted Job's request when the forty-two chapters of Job's harrowing experience were documented through the inspiration of the Holy Spirit. Job's account, to date, remains evergreen as it has provided succour and hope to many who have gone through trials and have come across the book of Job in the Bible.

Like Brother Jaiyeola and many others, Job's children died, and in chapter 19 verse 9, Job exclaimed to God, "He hath stopped me of my glory, and taken the crown from my head." But the climax of Job's lamentation is in job 13:15 when he surrendered to God's will and declared, "Though he slay me, yet will I TRUST in Him . . ."

While the Bible is a complete manual, the Lord today still inspires and has always inspired Christians in contemporary attestation to the recorded book of Job and that of the Christian faithful who may or will be going through such hard places. As I read through the pages of this inspired manual titled *The Gethsemane Prayer,* I was convinced that it has pleased the Lord to put the author through such hard grief, not because of himself alone, but for many who will find strength, faith, and courage as they pass through their trials and temptations. It is hoped that the Lord will bring Gethsemane to their memory and that they will surrender like Christ to God's perfect will and be a blessing to many others.

Again, as I watched on the internet the burial service of 'Manny' Mayowa Jaiyeola (Brother Femi's son) and the events afterward, it struck me that the Lord's beauty for the ashes was exceedingly displayed when the father, the author of this manual, found the courage to start distributing Gospel tracts to those that attended the sad event. I then deduced that doing His will is hard, but it could be most rewarding to find out that doing so can give us an assured place in Heaven at last. As you go through this manual, I pray that you will also find the courage to say, "Thy will be done, oh God," regardless of what you are passing through.

The author of this manual, Brother Olorunfemi Emmanuel Jaiyeola, a humble minister of Christ and a versatile academic whom I have related with as a mentor over some decades, remains a shrewd evangelist and a gospeler by his calling and inclinations. His coming to the limelight in the Apostolic Faith Church started during his famous leadership and team-led roles as national campus AVS president in the 90s.

Birthed by an Anglican Church priest and raised in the mission home where his father pastors, he grew up to experience what it means to surrender to the work of God, following his father to various towns and villages where they were transferred to as evangelists. He later found the gospel and got saved in the Apostolic Faith church at a young age. As he grew up in the church, he was admitted to the University and became a member of the then Campus AVS, now Apostolic Faith Campus Fellowship. During his years on campus, no one was left in doubt as to the call of God on him as a campus evangelist. He led a nationwide bombardment of campuses, winning souls for Christ. It is on record that God helped him to provide the strategy that revolutionized the ideas of many other young people moving with a vibrant 'Zion train' that cut across Nigerian higher institution campuses in the '90s.

As you read his inspirational piece, the hope of the late young 'Manny' and the hope of his consoled father is vividly expressed in Job 19: 25-26, that "my redeemer liveth, and that He shall stand at the latter day upon the earth: And though after my skin worms destroy this body, yet in my flesh, shall I see God."

How thankful are we, for certainly we shall see 'Manny' again.

*Isaac Adegbenga Aladegbola, PhD.*

*Crawford University Faith City, Ogun State Nigeria*

# Preface

This little book you are holding was born out of inspiration I got when my 22-year-old son, Emmanuel Oluwamayowa (fondly called Manny), passed into glory in his sleep on his college campus on September 23, 2022. When I got the shocking news on that memorable Friday at about 12 noon (PST), I was shattered and devastated.

That Friday gradually became bleak, gloomy, and cold as I saw my whole family enter a dark tunnel. The three of us—my wife, Maria; Josh, Manny's younger brother; and I—expressed grief differently. No one was with us in the first three hours, but Busayo (Manny's younger sister), who was in Athens, Georgia, and other extended family members joined us later by phone to mourn our loss. My siblings, especially, called in, wailing and weeping, and so we began a painful journey.

Saturday came and then Sunday; each day presenting different experiences. Reality was different from our dreams, but I still hung on to a very strong hope that something different would come our way.

My prayers rested on the fact that Jesus, being "the same yesterday, today, and forever" (Hebrews 13:8), would perform the needed miracle. What could be impossible for a good God? "Is there anything too hard for me, saith the Lord God" (Jeremiah 32:27). With these faith-boosting scriptures firmly rooted in my mind, I had the expectation of experiencing a 'Lazarus' miracle that would relieve me of the hopeless reality of Emmanuel's passing. Even after the call I made to the medical examiner's office in Baltimore, Maryland, the following Saturday afternoon that confirmed his death, I was still full of hope that the situation would be reversed.

Nights were like daytime; I was unable to sleep, and peace of mind eluded me. One night, as I lay on the bed with my memories of Emmanuel, imagining what he would have been doing on campus and how he would have been faring at that moment, I drifted off to sleep. I am not sure how long I slept, but when I began to awaken, I heard a gentle voice—the sweet voice of Jesus—say, "You have not prayed the Gethsemane prayer."

Immediately, my mind was refreshed and aligned with the idea of the agonizing prayer Jesus prayed with sweat like drops of blood. I thought that with this suggestion from Jesus, the expected miracle would happen. Immediately the voice said, "Gethsemane prayer is thy will be done." I had never heard this before. Although I know the Gethsemane story very well, in my journey as a Christian, I had never heard the phrase Gethsemane prayer. The message God was relaying suddenly dawned on me, and I got the inspiration for this book. "But there is a spirit in man: and the inspiration of the Almighty giveth them understanding" (Job 32:8).

My prayer, as you read and meditate on every line of this book, is that you will receive the understanding that the Lord expects of you as you surrender to His will through **the Gethsemane prayer.**

# The Gethsemane Prayer

*"Then cometh Jesus with them unto a place called Gethsemane, and saith unto the disciples, Sit ye here, while I go and pray yonder."*

**—Matthew 26:36, KJV**

There are many parts to the Gethsemane story. Most people remember Gethsemane as the garden where Jesus prayed and was arrested or where the disciples slept instead of spending time in prayer. **But there are significant lessons for us to learn from the events that**

**took place in this garden, which could be considered the beginning of the journey to the cross.**

Matthew and Mark clearly show that Jesus had a need to pray and was prepared to do so. He knew He had to pray because there was a burden to do so.

He knew where to pray, had a prayer point, and knew that God answers prayers. He knew the power in prayer and the victory that comes from prayer. He is God Himself. He was familiar with what works in the realm of the kingdom He shared with His Father. He understood human nature—the burdens, pains, and anxiety we encounter. Jesus appreciated the weakness of our flesh and the confusion it could cause to our spirit, and He also understood our grief. "For He knoweth our frame; He remembereth that we are dust" (Psalm 103:14). He knew how to overcome the fiery dart of the devil. He is God incarnate, but He put on flesh and so experienced how to overcome the flesh. He knew how to please the Father.

The Gethsemane prayer is not for 'bread and butter' provision. For this, Jesus did not need to pray an agonizing prayer. He would just have lifted up His eyes to Heaven to get that sorted out. But the Gethsemane prayer is deep.

It is a prayer of total surrender which aligns itself with the plan of omniscient God.

Because God is the Alpha, He knows the beginning from the end. He formed the world by His own wisdom and coordinates everything. He has ordained everything that will happen to us.

*"O Lord, our Lord, how excellent is thy name in all the earth! who hast set thy glory above the Heavens."*

—Psalm 8:1

*"When I consider thy Heavens, the work of thy fingers, the moon and the stars, which thou hast ordained."*

—Psalm 8:3

The plan of redemption brought Jesus to the world, and He knew it. The plan had been made from the foundation of the world (Rev. 13:8). Jesus declared this purpose in John 12:27 and John 18:37.

God's will was for Jesus to die on the cross in man's place so that He would save the world from the destruction planned for the devil and his angels. The will of God was settled.

Since blood must be shed for the remission of sins (Hebrews 9:22), it became necessary for Jesus to have blood in Him to pay the high price. Blood is life! "For the life of the flesh is in the blood: and I have given it to you upon the altar to make an atonement for your souls: for it is the blood that maketh an atonement for the soul" (Leviticus 17:11). Jesus needed to become human to experience our sensations and emotions. Hence the heart of man feels a heavy burden for what the flesh must bear. Jesus was made in our fashion (Philippians 2:8), so He could be a high priest that would be able to identify with our feelings. "For we have not an high priest which cannot be touched with the feeling of our infirmities; but was in all points tempted like as we are, yet without sin" (Hebrews 4:15).

The Gethsemane prayer is not a joke. It requires that we part ways with flesh and blood so that we can acknowledge and accept God's supreme will.

We cannot pray the Gethsemane prayer
without opening up to God about our fears,
unbelief, and self-will.

The Gethsemane prayer causes us to ascend unto the hills of consecration where we meet God's standard. This is what Jesus did by yielding the flesh to the will of God.

The Gethsemane prayer is simply THY WILL BE DONE.

CHAPTER 1

# What is Gethsemane?

*"And they came to a place which was named Gethsemane: and He saith to his disciples, Sit ye here, while I shall pray. And He taketh with Him Peter and James and John, and began to be sore amazed, and to be very heavy; And saith unto them, My soul is exceeding sorrowful unto death: tarry ye here, and watch. And He went forward a little, and fell on the ground, and prayed that, if it were possible, the hour might pass from Him. And He said, Abba, Father, all things are possible unto thee; take away this cup from me: nevertheless not what I will, but what thou wilt."*

**—Mark 14:32–36**

T he place called Gethsemane was where the savior retreated to have a conversation with God, the Abba Father, about His heavy heart.

It is also the place where we meet our Abba Father when our soul is exceedingly sorrowful unto death. Gethsemane is a place where we speak the truth about how our pains, fears, and troubles overwhelm us; a place where we uncover all the secrets in our hearts when no one except God sees and knows. The place called Gethsemane is where others will have to sit and watch us while we pray, where others could not help but sleep while our sweat and tears are hot and dripping like blood. It is the place where we will go a little further than usual—a little more time in agonizing prayers, a little more sacrifice, a little more fasting, a little more of everything.

Gethsemane was the place where
Jesus fell to the ground and prayed.

We would need, as we fall to the ground, to forget our status, reduce ourselves, and reposition ourselves spiritually. If the Son of God, God incarnate and second person in the Trinity, could fall to the ground to pray, would we who are flesh and blood do any less? No. We have to get to the place called Gethsemane and bow before Him "with whom we have to do" (Hebrews 4:13). For He sees and knows the intent of our heart. Gethsemane is where the will of man is weighed with the will of God, and we declare the intent of our heart honestly.

> Gethsemane is the place where the
> self is mortified.

It is a place where we need to go once and again and yet another time to seek the will and make the flesh yield to the will. It is where we need the assurance of the will, not a vain repetition, but the confirmation of yielding to the utmost will. In verse 39 of Mark 14, it says "And again he went away, and prayed, and spake the same words." Jesus did this not for ease nor for self-comfort but just to please God who is a spirit. Those who worship, serve, and live for Him must do it both in spirit and the truth. In the hymn *Close to Thee*, the songwriter says:

> Not for ease or worldly pleasure,
> Not for fame my prayer shall be;
> Gladly will I toil and suffer,
> Only let me walk with Thee.
> *Close to Thee, close to Thee,*
> *Close to Thee, close to Thee;*
> *Gladly will I toil and suffer,*
> *Only let me walk with Thee.*

At Gethsemane, we draw out the consecration to be closer to God and know His plans for us. We learn to understand what His design is for us and surrender to that design. It is a personal relationship. No one can help us pray it through. No one helped Jesus. His prayer partners were found asleep, their eyes heavy, not knowing what answer to give Him or words of support and encouragement to offer Him. This is what happens in Gethsemane, but surely God has all our answers. In the end, Jesus got the strength to overcome the flesh, and He got over the weakness, agony, and weariness. He got the victory that is only given when we meet Him in our Gethsemane.

Victory in Gethsemane is sure and universal.

It was sweet when God took me through the garden.

## CHAPTER 2

# Why Did Jesus Pray in Gethsemane?

*"And saith unto them, My soul is exceeding sorrowful unto death: tarry ye here, and watch. And he went forward a little, and fell on the ground, and prayed that, if it were possible, the hour might pass from Him. And he said, Abba, Father, all things are possible unto thee; take away this cup from me: nevertheless, not what I will, but what thou wilt. And he cometh, and findeth them sleeping, and saith unto Peter, Simon, sleepest thou? couldest not thou watch one hour? Watch ye and pray, lest ye enter into temptation. The spirit truly is ready, but the flesh is weak. And again he went away, and prayed, and spake the same words."*

**—Mark 14: 34-39**

D id Jesus need to pray the Gethsemane prayer? When Jesus came to Gethsemane, He was in the flesh with blood and water flowing in Him. He took upon Himself the nature of man, so He knew our pains and emotional trauma and felt the burden of what lay ahead of Him.

Let us look closely at who Jesus was before He got to Gethsemane. Jesus is the second person in the Trinity. He is the Word that God spoke at the creation of the world (John 1:1; Genesis 1:1, 2; Colossians 1:16). At the creation of man, God the Father called a council, the Trinity, and said "Let us make man in our image," that is, the divine soul. The Trinity does not have physical bodies—flesh and blood.

At the fall of man, sinless blood was needed for atonement. This necessitated the recurring symbolic process of shedding the blood of unblemished animals during the Levitical period. This practice was instituted by God for the children of Israel through the time of the prophets and kings. However, a sacred Lamb had been slain from the foundation of the world (Rev.13:8) to take away the sins of the whole world; this was the only begotten Son of God (John 3:16). John saw in his revelation that there was no one in Heaven or earth who was able to open the book, but the Lion of the tribe of Judah, the Lamb of God, prevailed (Revelation 5:3–9), and this stirred up great joy in Heaven.

> Jesus knew the purpose for
> which He came into the world;
> His coming was not an accident.

He knew the will and plan of God. Being divine, He did not have blood to shed, so Jesus had to humble Himself and take the form of a man (Philippians 2:7). He was conceived, nurtured in the womb, and eventually born in the flesh so that He could dwell among us (John 1:14).

In the flesh, He was able to live like us. He was tempted and tried but remained without sin.

He also experienced our weaknesses, as shown in the garden of Gethsemane.

In the garden, the flesh manifested, and Jesus desired that the will of God be altered, just as we oftentimes desire ourselves. The flesh wanted to respond to the negative situation by seeking a way of escape. Don't we do the same? Jesus went to Gethsemane and enlisted His disciples to pray with and for Him. When our flesh sinks deep into looking for a way of escape and respite, have we ever felt the need to get to Gethsemane to seek the will of God? When we are faced with the struggle between yielding to the divine will or the desire of the flesh, the pressure we undergo could make us sweat profusely. Self manifested itself at the moment when Jesus said, "Let this cup pass from me," and His soul was sorrowful unto death. The Son of God knew why He had to come to the world before He even left the throne, but here was the flesh trying to strike a deal and negotiate with God concerning the eternal plan.

Jesus never lived His life in consultation with flesh and blood, and that was why after a 40- day fast in the wilderness, He overcame Satan's temptations. The Bible tells us that He was hungry and the flesh was weak, but the inner man was strong. Jesus once declared to Peter that flesh and blood did not reveal His divinity to Him. He lives in the spirit with His Father. The prayer in John 17 attests to this. His desire was to glorify His Father, but when human nature perceived the weight of the ultimate price, flesh and blood responded with fear.

Our victory lies in bowing to the will of God. When we get into our Gethsemane space and season, may God help us to deploy His grace within us in order to deny self and wholly accept that God's will be done.

## CHAPTER 3

# How Do We Pray the Gethsemane Prayer?

*"After this manner therefore pray ye: Our Father which art in Heaven, Hallowed be thy name. Thy kingdom come, Thy will be done in earth, as it is in Heaven."*

**—Matthew 6:9-10**

L et's cast our minds back to the prayer model Jesus taught His disciples in Matthew 6:9–13. One of the key points in that prayer is similar to the Gethsemane prayer—Thy will be done on earth as it is in Heaven.

The Gethsemane prayer is not just a model for us to use here on earth, it also prepares us, as God's children, for life in Heaven. Jesus said, "Not my will," even though He is the second person in the Holy Trinity and has authority in Heaven and on earth (Matthew 28:18).

"Wherefore God also hath highly exalted Him and given Him a name which is above every name: That at the name of Jesus every knee should bow, of things in Heaven, and things in earth, and things under the earth; And that every tongue should confess that Jesus Christ is Lord, to the glory of God the Father" (Philippians 2:9–11). Jesus has control in Heaven and on earth and below the earth. He could have had His way, but at Gethsemane, He demonstrated implicit obedience to the Word which He taught His disciples. He had taught them to do the will of God. In John 7, He told them about knowing and doing this will: "If any man will do his will, he shall know of the doctrine, whether it be of God, or whether I speak of myself" (John 7:17).

> The Gethsemane prayer
> overrules our will.

As children of God, we are not to live based on our will and desires, neither should we attempt to travel the Christian journey by our self-designed rules and protocols.

Ideally, we subject our intellect and ability to the instruction manual of any operative machine we use; otherwise, we endanger ourselves and the equipment. If you fly an airplane as a pilot, crew member, or passenger, there are safety measures designed by the manufacturer of the airplane in conformity to the world's standards on aviation which you need to comply with in order to have a successful flight. No category of users would operate based on their willful choice without exposing the flight to serious danger and adverse consequences. Everyone submits to the directives of the operations manual in order to be safe.

The will of God for Christians is not
negotiable if we desire a place where the total
will of God is the order—Heaven.

Heaven is a place with perfect orderliness, so we must start to practice how to live there by yielding ourselves to the will of God here below. The world today is in chaos because everyone promotes their will and selfish interest; people go their different ways. This is confirmed in the book of prophet Isaiah, "All we like sheep have gone astray; we have turned every one to his own way" (Isaiah 53:6). When people with different wills go their different ways without recourse to a central coordinator—God— anarchy and disorderliness set in. Is that not what the world looks like today? Heaven cannot accommodate any other will and way apart from God's. We must submit to God's will.

Jesus' flesh was weak, and this weakness caused Him to make a request that the cup of sacrificial death be passed away from Him, but He ultimately surrendered. If Jesus had not surrendered His will, what would have been the hope of redemption? Who would have done the work? Where would the victory over death and its sting for the saints have been? How would we have had the blood—the pure blood—to cleanse, heal, and give deliverance? Who would have vanquished hell and the devil? How would the promise of crushing the head of the devil that God made in Eden have been fulfilled? Ha! The whole world would have been plunged into a devastating calamity. We thank God Jesus went to Gethsemane and surrendered His will. The Gethsemane prayer is "not as I will. . . ." We have many plans and desires, and sometimes we draw plans for ourselves and our family members, but God's will is supreme.

I had my will and desire for my dear son. He has as part of his name Emmanuel Olorunfemi—we shared these names. I preferred him not to go by Junior but rather as Emmanuel II. When he matured enough to understand, I told him how I wanted him to bear and carry the name forward. He was to be addressed as Emmanuel Jaiyeola II, and each time I saw this, I was pleased because I thought we were creating a chain of history. He understood he would have Emmanuel Jaiyeola III, but that was not the will of God. I had to bow. Whatever may be our plans and desires, we must know that God has His own will for us, and whatever the will of God is, we know it is for our good because His thoughts and plans for us are always good (Jeremiah 29:11). That is why Paul admonished us that, "In every thing give thanks: for this is the will of God in Christ Jesus concerning you" (I Thessalonians 5:18). We need to seek, know, and do the will of God. That was Jesus' example. "Not as I will, but as Thou wilt." The will of God is the secret map to our victory. The will of God brings us into God's incorruptible inheritance.

"Not my will. . . ." This is not a sign of weakness but a total recognition of the sovereignty of God in directing our lives.

The will of God is not centered on what benefits us alone; it is beyond us. It is not all about our interest.

The will of God is not selfish
and self-centered.

God looks beyond us. God is love, and He works out His will in our lives to help and care for people we may not know and cannot by our own finite minds and resources reach out to. In His bid to cater to the needs of some people or to rescue some others from the clutches of the devil, He performs His will in our lives.

The memorial service held for my son gave many people the opportunity to repent and have a change of heart. The service was live cast, and by the second day, over 3,000 views had been recorded—and some may have watched in groups. This figure excludes those who were physically in attendance. The sermon and songs reached out to many who, naturally, would not have attended a church service to hear the sound Gospel message preached. I believe some people must have given their lives to Jesus in their private corners. This was confirmed by a call I got from someone in Nigeria who said, "I watched the service live, and I rededicated my life to God."

God brings His will to pass in our lives to bless others. Someone, somewhere, may find encouragement through our experience at a time when the "heart is exceedingly sorrowful." If we flash our minds back to the many ways we give up our own way of doing things to ensure safety, not necessarily for ourselves alone, then we would appreciate how God can turn our unpleasant experiences—His will—into a source of blessing for other people. We should, therefore, thank God even when we do not understand His will.

> His will transcends the present,
> and it is usually not clear to us
> why it prevails over ours.

Jesus yielded His will to God's will, and that marked the fulfillment of everlasting victory for all races and ages.

## CHAPTER 4

# His Will is our Peace and Heritage

*"The law of the LORD is perfect, converting the soul: the testimony of the LORD is sure, making wise the simple. The statutes of the LORD are right, rejoicing the heart: the commandment of the LORD is pure, enlightening the eyes. The fear of the LORD is clean, enduring for ever: the judgments of the LORD are true and righteous altogether. More to be desired are they than gold, yea, than much fine gold: sweeter also than honey and the honeycomb. Moreover by them is thy servant warned: and in keeping of them there is great reward."*

**—Psalm 19: 7-11**

A standard way of showing and knowing we have surrendered to God's will is obeying and acting according to what He demands of us.

"In every thing give thanks: for this is the will of God in Christ Jesus concerning you" (1 Thessalonians 5:18). God's will is His heritage for all His children.

"Behold, what manner of love the Father hath bestowed upon us, that we should be called the sons of God" (1 John 3:1). Therefore, as sons and daughters, we have an entitlement to His estate. He thinks and plans well for us.

If we have surrendered our lives and all to God and He has adopted us into His family as sons and daughters through the blood of Jesus, 1 John 3:2 expressly says, "Beloved, now are we the sons of God, and it doth not yet appear what we shall be: but we know that, when He shall appear, we shall be like Him; for we shall see Him as He is."

God is serious about His responsibility
to take care of us and supply all our needs
now and in the future.

If we believe and know that God is a good Father, then we rest assured that whatever He does or permits to happen to us is from His good plans and thoughts toward us (Jeremiah 29:11). I had fantastic plans for Emmanuel, as any good father would have for his son. One of the latest plans we both shared was for him to quit his campus part-time job, focus on his major, and search for internships or jobs along his professional line, with the aim of getting more experience to enable him to sit for certification examinations. I also planned to buy him a decent car, which he would be able to maintain without recourse to me after securing a better job. Good plans? Yes. But they never materialized because God, the supreme Father, had different plans for both of us. Emmanuel gratefully accepted my plans. He shared the idea with people around him, and he started looking for a professional job after quitting menial campus jobs.

Just as I had plans for Emmanuel, my son,

God also has plans for us through Jesus Christ
who paid for our adoption into His family.

29

We are expected to give thanks. Again, 1 Thessalonians remind us, "In every thing give thanks: for this is the will of God in Christ Jesus concerning you." The will of God must prevail in every area of our lives as God's children. Since we become Christ's at the point of salvation, our will is turned over to Him. We are His children, and He brings His will to pass in our lives. A good child of God accepts His will just as a good child obeys his parent. Children of God live in obedience to God's will, and that obedience is expressed when we thank Him in everything that comes our way.

If we believe He has good plans and thoughts for us and have faith in His Word, we will obey. No child of God lives in disobedience. We have a desire to abide by His will—His sovereign will— and not our will.

God's way and His will are inseparable. We must walk in His way as the hymn, *Trust and Obey,* below says:

> When we walk with the Lord
> In the light of His word
> What a glory He sheds on our way!

While we do His good will,

He abides with us still,

And with all who will trust and obey.

Trust and obey,

For there is no other way

To be happy in Jesus

But to trust and obey.

When we do this, we find joy, happiness, and peace, for submitting to His will is our peace.

When an estate is bequeathed to children, a will guides the administration of the inheritance. The executor of the will administers the will according to its content. The will is usually for the testator's family and whatever cause the owner of the estate is interested in. The content of the will is binding only on those whom the testator cares for. Similarly, our Heavenly Father's will is meant for those whom He cares for, His sons and daughters.

"The Spirit itself beareth witness with our spirit, that we are the children of God" (Romans 8:16). Since we have this spiritual birth certificate that connects us with God, we have a share in the inheritance with His beloved Son, Jesus Christ.

"And if children, then heirs; heirs of God, and joint-heirs with Christ; if so be that we suffer with him, that we may be also glorified together" (Romans 8:17). We indeed have a share in the will, of which the Gethsemane prayer is a part. Jesus surrendered and said, "Not my will, but thine, be done" (Luke 22:42).

> Sometimes, we find ourselves in hard places where God's will does not correspond with our desires or expectations.

My wife and I have thoughts and plans for all our children. We love and cherish them. We have also made many sacrifices and prayed much for them to serve the Lord and grow up to become adults who will contribute positively to society. We eagerly looked forward to seeing Manny graduate from college, but contrary to our desires, God allowed us to pass through a seemingly bitter experience. One Sunday, three weeks after Manny passed away, when I had the opportunity to preach, God told me clearly to say "in every thing give thanks: for this is the WILL of God in Christ Jesus" for me. My response was, "God help me. Just as you helped Jesus in the garden, please help me to say, 'Thy will be done.'"

## CHAPTER 5

# How Do We Pray Concerning the Will of God?

*"And it came to pass, that, as he was praying in a certain place, when he ceased, one of his disciples said unto Him, Lord, teach us to pray, as John also taught his disciples. And he said unto them, When ye pray, say, Our Father which art in Heaven, Hallowed be thy name. Thy kingdom come. Thy will be done, as in Heaven, so in earth."*

**—Luke 11: 1-2**

From the various examples and admonitions found in the Bible, we know we ought to surrender our will to God. But we also know that the spirit and the flesh are in a constant struggle to do the will of God. "For the flesh lusteth against the Spirit, and the Spirit against the flesh: and these are contrary the one to the other: so that ye cannot do the things that ye would" (Galatians 5:17).

As Matthew 26:41 reminds us, "The spirit indeed is willing, but the flesh is weak." When we find ourselves in this struggle, just as our Lord experienced in the garden, we need to agonize in prayer. And we thank God that Jesus walked the path before us and knows our weaknesses. He is a sympathizing Savior who helps us in our infirmities.

During the first few days of my bereavement, I drew strength from a song that kept ringing in my heart. It was a song my dad used to sing in my childhood days, and I sometimes heard it in church services. The song had a solemn meaning to me as I grew up, and I see it now as an encouragement to all.

May God give us the grace to pray like the songwriter has in the hymn *My God, my Father, While I Stray*:

> My God my father while I stray,
>
> Far from home, on life's rough way
>
> Oh teach me from my heart to say,
>
> **Thy will be done.**
>
> Though dark my path and sad my lot,
>
> Let me be still and murmur not,
>
> Or breathe the prayer divinely taught,
>
> **Thy will be done.**
>
> What though in lonely grief I sigh
>
> For friends beloved, no longer nigh,
>
> Submissive still would I reply,
>
> **Thy will be done.**
>
> If Thou should'st call me to resign
>
> What most I prize, it ne'er was mine
>
> I only yield Thee what is thine;
>
> **Thy Will be done**

Let but my fainting heart be blest

With Thy sweet Spirit for its guest

May God, to Thee I leave the rest

**Thy will be done**

Renew my will from day to day,

Blend it with Thine and take away

All that now makes it hard to say

**Thy will be done**

Then, when on earth I breathe no more

The prayer, oft mix'd with tears before,

I'll sing upon a happier shore,

**Thy will be done.**

The Gethsemane prayer—Thy will be done—though usually hard to accept, should be our heart's cry.

## CHAPTER 6

# Even in Little Decisions, There is Greater Victory in Asking and Doing His Will

*"I delight to do thy will, O my God: yea, thy law is within my heart."*

**—Psalm 40:8**

A s I was concluding this writing, a deep thought came into my heart during one of my studies. How many decisions do we make daily, and how many of these are made according to the will of God? How often do we seek the will of God in each of those decisions?

The decisions may be as little as what clothes I should put on. Yes, we may think that is too insignificant to bother the great God about. Moreover, He has bestowed on us His wisdom generously to take some initiatives. Yes, that is true, but in my deep meditation, I see that our decisions and choices should be the will of God. This is true not only on big issues or things that are of greater interest to us or that we struggle with, but also as children of God, our lives at any point in time should be about our God and whatever we do should glorify Him. As is stated in 1 Corinthians 10: 31, **"Whether therefore ye eat, or drink, or whatsoever ye do, do all to the glory of God."**

We must do all to the glory of God, and for this to happen, we must be seeking His will in whatever we do.

We should not stop asking God and listening to Him on those steps, little and big, before we take them. In our responses to situations, as His people, we should seek the will of God concerning each.

1 Thessalonians 5:18 reminds us, "In every thing give thanks; for this is the will of God in Christ Jesus concerning you." Did I just read "every thing'? Yes, every thing! God has a will for us. Once we turn over our lives to Him, how do we seek and know His will concerning everything about us? We study the word. Since there are some basic rules we know according to His word, we should not be asking what is laid out already. In His word, some of His principles are clearly written. These are His will. If we desire to please Him in our ways and do His will, we will not question those basic principles or interpret them with our own ideas. We live to please Him who has bought us with a price. Our delight should be as Psalm 40: 8 says, "I delight to do thy will, O my God: yea, thy law is within my heart."

If we live in His spirit,

we will be guided and led by His Spirit.

Romans 8:14 reveals, "For as many as are led by the spirit of God, they are the sons of God." The spirit will nudge, speak, direct, and warn us. If we are truly willing to obey and do His will, we will just say, "I surrender all." Even though the closest person to us may not be going the same way, God's spirit will ever be clear to you on what He demands from you. If we truly want to give glory in everything we do, we will keep His commandments.

The victory we have is in knowing and doing the will of God. Jesus provided the example by knowing and doing the will of God in Gethsemane. He has prepared for us victory and peace which passes the understanding of any therapist or therapeutical assistance. We will experience a life of total peace if we seek and follow His will in all we do. His will is never to our detriment, but to our good. In the long run, it is also to the benefit of others close, far, and perhaps even many generations to come. His will in our lives signifies His trust in us and what He plans for us. His plans are for good. What a contrary opinion to our flesh when it comes up with the fear and anxiety of what ifs! We must keep our focus on the Lord who has established a covenant with us at salvation. God will bring out from our little and big experiences sweet victories for us and others.

Let us be willing to seek and delight to do His will in all ways like the psalmist in Psalm 40:8 who says, "I delight to do thy will."

## CHAPTER 7

# The Wonders of Surrendering to His Will

*"Then he said unto them, Go your way, eat the fat, and drink the sweet, and send portions unto them for whom nothing is prepared: for this day is holy unto our Lord: neither be ye sorry; for the joy of the Lord is your strength."*

**—Nehemiah 8:10**

**W**hile passing through the seemingly dark days, I saw that God, who had prepared a greater will for me, never left me to the wiles of the devil. The Holy Spirit, our comforter and guide, was always ready to give me portions of the scriptures that answer each moment of questions. Through the agency of the Holy Spirit, who interprets the Word perfectly, He pours His oil to soothe my heart whenever there is a pain. The Lord walked beside me through the shadows and valley of fears and worries. He preached to me a sermon about believing His own report from the book of Isaiah chapter 53 verse 1. I know God is close, and He is real, but He made Himself closer and more real at those moments. Truly, God is omnipresent. He talks at the right time, and He "bid my anxious fear subside." He never leaves me alone.

He provides strength. The power of the Bible is real. The workings of its words keep me going. When I am weak, He drops a scripture into my heart to quench the fiery dart of the devil.

The Lord inspired my heart with Philippians 4:6, which says, "Be careful for nothing..." This verse made me understand that I should not permit thoughts and questions about my son's death to bother me again. I should let go and free my heart of what I cannot change. It is needless to ask or worry. I think that is a good approach to God's will. When He has made His will known to us and we accept it, it is improper and a sign of loss of faith in God to move around with a burdened heart and a sullen look. The enemy of our soul works to lay a weight on our hearts to take away our sleep and peace. The rest of Philippians 4:6 says, "in every thing by prayer and supplication with thanksgiving let your requests be made known unto God." The Lord says in every thing. Yes, you read that correctly. I did this. I laid bare before Him how confused and tired I was, and the Lord struck me with a gong-like awareness one evening. The burden vanished, the pain left, and the devil was disgraced.

The antidote for worry is praise.

When we accept the will of God, we don't only say yes, we also move to the next and better level of praising Him for His will. This antidote brings unto us a graceful time and is also the flight that takes us to the presence of God continually. We find the fullness of joy in the presence of the Lord, and the joy of the Lord is our strength. From the day I had an encounter with the Lord, I began to live in full strength and joy.

Accepting the will of God is one of the "every thing" Philippians speaks of which is taken before Him with thanksgiving. Therein lies our joy, which is eternal and incorruptible. The Lord has done that which He pleases. With this, I am confidently obeying the word of Nehemiah that I should go and eat, drink, and share the hope I have in Jesus and His resurrection. Jesus told me my son is in paradise, and He chose to take him when he had lived his full life. God revealed to me that He owns him. He only loaned him to me, and He has taken his possession. There was no bargain with me on when He would take what He gave me to watch over. I thanked Him for giving me the privilege to have Manny for

22 years. I look forward to the next opportunity to do more for Him. Nehemiah said I should not be sorry but rather let His joy be my strength.

> If we abide in that obedience and joy,
> we shall have all-around strength
> to attain victory.

I am thankful that each experience allows us to know and walk closer with God leaving us better Christians, not bitter ones, if we accept with thanksgiving His divine will.

*The joy of the Lord is your strength.*

# Have You Prayed Gethsemane's Prayer?

*"...men ought always to pray, and not to faint..."*
**—Luke 18:1**

I f you have not prayed the Gethsemane prayer, maybe you have not gone to the garden. Maybe you have not identified your Gethsemane, or the time has not come for you to shed the flesh and let the spirit be quickened? Yes, the spirit is willing, but the flesh is weak. Perhaps you have not accepted the cup as the will of God? Maybe you wish the cup to pass according to your desires.

If this is the case, then it is time to ask where the glory of God is in this. Ask yourself if you have really thought of perfect obedience to His word without any reservation. If this is the spot we have found ourselves in, then it is time to go to the garden.

It is time to pray the Gethsemane prayer with our hearts opened with obedience and say, "Thy will be done."

> The Gethsemane prayer
> will put us in the presence of
> God with angels ministering
> unto us as victors.

The Gethsemane prayer brings blessings eternal to many beyond our reach. Myriads of people from many generations have been tremendously blessed with the Gethsemane experience of Job and the total surrender of his will to God, to the shame of the devil and the glory of God.

When we surrender our will, God is proud of such a child, and the devil is completely defeated under our feet by Christ Jesus who won the victory for us. Then we inherit the kingdom that has been secured for us from the foundation of the world.

John 14: 1- 3 tells us of the promised inheritance for overcomers. 1 Cor. 2: 9 explains the inestimable return on investment on all who just signed the blank check and commit it into the hands of the Heavenly king in His vast dominion.

Gethsemane's prayer kills flesh but glorifies God.

Jesus is our perfect example.

Pray it today. Pray it tomorrow. Pray it every day. It draws us to the unique relationship with God only to please Him and be a blessing. Just as the words of the hymn *Thou, My Everlasting Portion* remind us:

> *Lead me through the vale of shadows,*
> *Bear me o'er life's fitful sea;*

*Then the gate of life eternal*
*May I enter, Lord, with Thee.*
*Close to Thee, close to Thee,*
*Close to Thee, close to Thee;*
*Then the gate of life eternal*
*May I enter, Lord, with Thee.*

Will you start praying Gethsemane prayer today? Let us do it!

# ABOUT THE AUTHOR

Olorunfemi (Femi) Emmanuel Jaiyeola PhD. is a minister of Christ and an academic. His father was an Anglican priest, and Femi was raised in the mission home where his father pastored. He grew up watching his father preach in the various towns and villages where he was sent as an evangelist. Femi later found Christ for himself and was saved in the Apostolic Faith in his teenage years. He later attended university and became a member and served as the president of the Campus AVS, now known as Apostolic Faith Campus Fellowship. Through this, his faith in God grew and influenced many. Femi, with his colleagues, was instrumental in winning souls to Christ on campuses across Nigeria.

# ACKNOWLEDGMENT

I want to acknowledge the support and the works of the Holy Spirit in all the times of preparation of this book. It was not my intention or plan, as you would know and agree with me. This is absolutely the Lord's WILL. Not my plan. He did and directed and led to all who worked on this book. This is according to His WILL. I have never met the publisher nor read about them, But He just led me to them. All who did one thing or the other were His choice. I am very grateful to God for the leading of the Holy Spirit. He is real. Thank you all for your prayers, even though you may not know how God is answering them, but He does and still doing. I use this time to say Thank you for all the human support received during the time we passed through this experience, May the blessings of God be upon everyone but we know that God is too good to do evil. The WILL of God will bless us beyond now.